MW01233218

DISCARD

THE LIFE OF
SUSAN B. ANTHONY

BY ELIZABETH RAUM

AMICUS | AMICUS INK

Sequence is published by Amicus and Amicus Ink
P.O. Box 1329, Mankato, MN 56002
www.amicuspublishing.us

Library of Congress Cataloging-in-Publication Data
Names: Raum, Elizabeth, author.
Title: The life of Susan B. Anthony / by Elizabeth Raum.
Description: Mankato, Minnesota : Amicus, 2019. | Series: Sequence Change Maker
  Biographies | Includes index.
Identifiers: LCCN 2018031883 (print) | LCCN 2018032715 (ebook) | ISBN
  9781681517636 (pdf) | ISBN 9781681516813 (library binding) | ISBN
  9781681524672 (pbk.)
Subjects: LCSH: Anthony, Susan B. (Susan Brownell), 1820-1906--Juvenile literature. |
  Suffragists--United States--Biography--Juvenile literature. | Feminists--United States--
  Biography--Juvenile literature. | Women social reformers--United States--Biography--
  Juvenile literature. | Women's rights--United States--Juvenile literature.
Classification: LCC HQ1413.A55 (ebook) | LCC HQ1413.A55 R38 2019 (print) | DDC
  305.4209 [B] --dc23
LC record available at https://lccn.loc.gov/2018031883

Editor: Alissa Thielges
Designer: Ciara Beitlich
Photo Researcher: Holly Young

Photo Credits: WikiCommons/LSE Library cover; WikiCommons/G.E. Perine & Co. cover; WikiCommons/Internet Archive Book Images 5; WikiCommons/Tichnor Bros. Inc., 6–7; Library of Congress/Currier and Ives 9; Library of Congress/anti-slavery society 10; WikiCommons/Bradley & Ralofson, S.F. 10; WikiCommons 12, 21, 26–27; Getty/Bettmann 12–13, 25; WikiCommons/Napoleon Sarony 14–15; Library of Congress/Harris & Ewing, photographer 17; Mary Evans/Ny Illustrerad Tidning 18–19; Library of Congress/Edmonston, Washington, D.C. 20–21; Flickr/TradingCardsNPS 22; Getty/Stock Montage 29

Printed in the United States of America

HC 10 9 8 7 6 5 4 3 2 1
PB 10 9 8 7 6 5 4 3 2 1

Who was Susan B. Anthony?

In the 1800s, women in the United States had few rights. They could not own property or speak at public meetings. Women were not allowed to vote. Married women could not hold jobs. Susan B. Anthony dreamed of women having the same rights as men. She devoted her life to making that happen.

Susan fought for equal rights for women.

Susan and her six siblings grew up in this house in Adams, Massachusetts.

Susan B. Anthony is born.

FEB. 15, 1820

LOADING . . . LOADING . . .

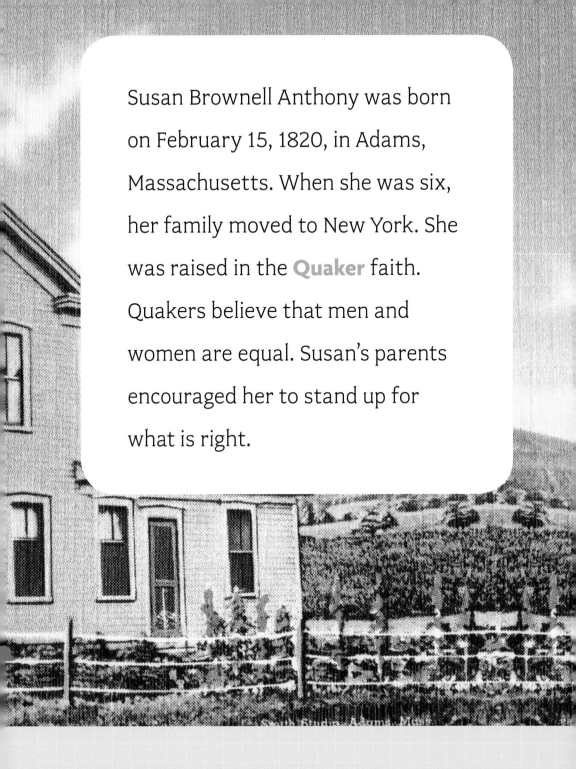

Susan Brownell Anthony was born on February 15, 1820, in Adams, Massachusetts. When she was six, her family moved to New York. She was raised in the **Quaker** faith. Quakers believe that men and women are equal. Susan's parents encouraged her to stand up for what is right.

LOADING... LOADING... LOADING...

Facing Unequal Treatment

In 1845, her family moved to Rochester, New York. Susan taught school nearby. Most women her age got married. Susan chose not to. This way, she had more time to help others. She joined a **temperance** group. They worked to ban alcohol. Susan gave speeches about it. At the time, few women spoke in public. That didn't stop Susan.

Susan B. Anthony is born.

FEB. 15, 1820   1845   DING...LOADING...

Susan gives speeches about temperance.

The temperance movement was known as the Holy War. This drawing shows women fighting for the cause.

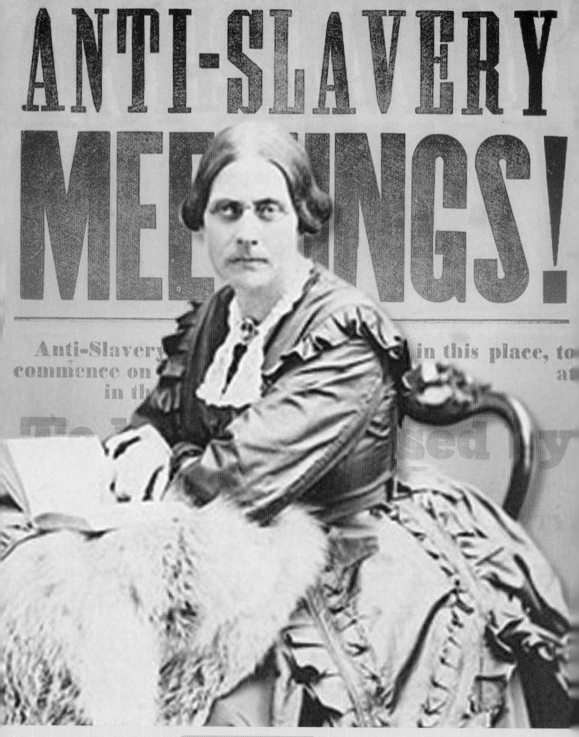

Susan joins anti-slavery group and teacher's union.

Susan B. Anthony is born.

FEB. 15, 1820   1845   1848   . . . L O A D I N G . . .

Susan gives speeches about temperance.

In 1848, Susan learned that male teachers were paid $10.00 a week. She earned only $2.50. It wasn't fair. She joined a teacher's **union**. She pushed for equal pay. She also joined an anti-slavery group. Soon after, she quit teaching. She wanted to focus on helping others. She rallied others to her causes.

Susan often hosted anti-slavery groups in her home.

LOADING...LOADING...LOADING...

WOMEN'S EMANCIPATION PETITION.

☞ Put no signatures on the back of the Petition.
☞ When this sheet is full, paste another at the bottom.
☞ If possible, send us contributions to help pay the heavy expenses incurred at this office.
☞ Do not copy the names—return the original signatures ; no matter if the paper is worn or soiled.
☞ When your district is thoroughly convassed, return the petitions and donations to this office.
☞ Address SUSAN B. ANTHONY, Secretary, U. S. National League, Room 20, Cooper Institute, New York.

To the Senate and House of Representatives of the United States :

The Undersigned, Women of the United States above the age of eighteen years, earnestly pray that your Honorable Body will pass, at the earliest practicable day, an Act emancipating all persons of African descent held to involuntary service or labor in the United States.

NAME.	RESIDENCE.
Eliza Williams	Seneca Nemeha Co Kansas
Rhoda Woodealf	Ouacuck Nemaha Co Kansas
Ellen Divine	"
Lizzie S. Fuller	Seneca Nemeha Co Kansas
M. C. Pickham	"
H. A. Flower	"
Lizzie W. Pelton	"
Mary A. Burnes	"
Amanda M. Sappin	"

Susan B. Anthony is born.

Susan joins anti-slavery group and teacher's union.

FEB. 15, 1820   **1845**   **1848**   **JULY 1848**   OADING . . .

Susan gives speeches about temperance.

Seneca Falls Convention is held; Susan begins to fight for women's rights.

12

On July 19, 1848, the first meeting for women's rights was held. It was called the Seneca Falls **Convention**. Elizabeth Cady Stanton planned it. Susan did not go, but she read about it in a newspaper. By this time, she was already working to ban alcohol, end slavery, and improve teacher pay. She added another cause: women's rights.

Susan and Elizabeth started a **petition** to end slavery. Over 400,000 women signed it.

LOADING... LOADING... LOADING...

Susan met Elizabeth Stanton in May 1851. They soon became close friends. In 1852, Susan attended a temperance convention in Rochester, New York. She wanted to take part. She rose to speak but was told to sit down and listen. Only men could speak. So Susan left. She vowed to make changes.

Susan (right) and Elizabeth (left) were lifelong friends.

Susan B. Anthony is born.

Susan joins anti-slavery group and teacher's union.

| FEB. 15, 1820 | 1845 | 1848 | JULY 1848 |

Susan gives speeches about temperance.

Seneca Falls Convention is held; Susan begins to fight for women's rights.

Taking Action

In September 1852, Susan attended a women's rights convention in Syracuse, New York. Elizabeth spoke about women's **suffrage**. This is the right for women to vote. Elizabeth encouraged Susan to join the fight. Susan agreed. She began giving speeches. She talked about women's suffrage.

Men look at posters from a group that was against women's right to vote.

Susan B. Anthony is born.

Susan joins anti-slavery group and teacher's union.

Susan hears Elizabeth speak; gives speeches for women's suffrage.

FEB. 15, 1820   1845   1848   JULY 1848   SEPT. 1852

Susan gives speeches about temperance.

Seneca Falls Convention is held; Susan begins to fight for women's rights.

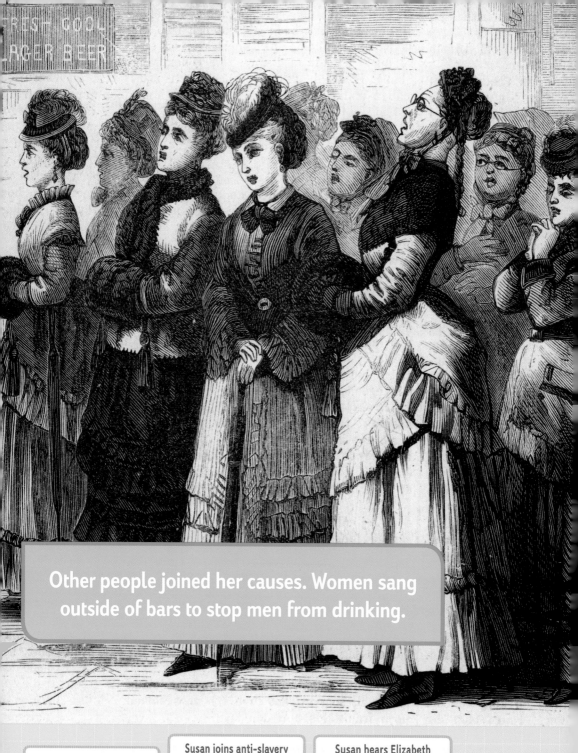

Other people joined her causes. Women sang outside of bars to stop men from drinking.

Susan B. Anthony is born.

Susan joins anti-slavery group and teacher's union.

Susan hears Elizabeth speak; gives speeches for women's suffrage.

FEB. 15, 1820   1845   1848   JULY 1848   SEPT. 1852   1853

Susan gives speeches about temperance.

Seneca Falls Convention is held; Susan begins to fight for women's rights.

Susan works for women's property rights and suffrage.

Susan did not give up her other causes. She still spoke against slavery and worked for better teacher pay. She spoke to large crowds. People listened to her ideas. Newspapers reported what she said. She met with lawmakers, too. In 1853, Susan went door-to-door with petitions. She asked people to support suffrage for all and married women's right to own property.

Progress was slow. Many people disagreed with Susan. But she kept fighting. In 1868, she and Elizabeth formed the American Equal Rights Association. They began a newspaper called *The Revolution*. They wrote about women's rights. They pushed for shorter hours and better wages for workers. Susan wrote about women who were farmers, dentists, and inventors.

Susan and Elizabeth wrote *The Revolution* together.

VOL. I.—N

The I

NATI

Susan B. Anthony is born.

Susan joins anti-slavery group and teacher's union.

Susan hears Elizabeth speak; gives speeches for women's suffrage.

| FEB. 15, 1820 | 1845 | 1848 | JULY 1848 | SEPT. 1852 | 1853 |

Susan gives speeches about temperance.

Seneca Falls Convention is held; Susan begins to fight for women's rights.

Susan works for women's property rights and suffrage.

Susan publishes *The Revolution* with Elizabeth.

1868

LOADING... LOADING...

African-American men cast their votes after the constitution changed in 1869.

Susan B. Anthony is born.

Susan joins anti-slavery group and teacher's union.

Susan hears Elizabeth speak; gives speeches for women's suffrage.

FEB. 15, 1820   1845   1848   JULY 1848   SEPT. 1852   1853

Susan gives speeches about temperance.

Seneca Falls Convention is held; Susan begins to fight for women's rights.

Susan works for women's property rights and suffrage.

Risking Prison

On February 26, 1869, Congress passed the 15th **Amendment**. It gave all male citizens over age 21 the right to vote. Susan wanted it to include women. Lawmakers did not agree. African-American men could now vote. Women of any race still could not. That year, Susan gave about 100 speeches on women's rights.

Susan publishes *The Revolution* with Elizabeth.

1868   FEBRUARY 26, 1869   DING . . . LOADING . . .

Congress passes 15th Amendment: all males can vote.

Susan knew talk wasn't enough. In 1872, she took a bold step. She went to the **polls** and voted. It was a presidential election. Newspapers all over the country reported on this. Two weeks later, she was arrested. On December 23, 1872, she was fined $500. She never paid it.

This drawing makes fun of Susan voting and women's rights. It is called "The Woman Who Dared."

Susan B. Anthony is born.

Susan joins anti-slavery group and teacher's union.

Susan hears Elizabeth speak; gives speeches for women's suffrage.

| FEB. 15, 1820 | 1845 | 1848 | JULY 1848 | SEPT. 1852 | 1853 |

Susan gives speeches about temperance.

Seneca Falls Convention is held; Susan begins to fight for women's rights.

Susan works for women's property rights and suffrage.

Susan publishes *The Revolution* with Elizabeth.

Susan is arrested for voting.

1868   FEBRUARY 26, 1869   1872   . . . L O A D I N G . . .

Congress passes 15th Amendment: all males can vote.

Susan B. Anthony is born.

Susan joins anti-slavery group and teacher's union.

Susan hears Elizabeth speak; gives speeches for women's suffrage.

FEB. 15, 1820   1845   1848   JULY 1848   SEPT. 1852   1853

Susan gives speeches about temperance.

Seneca Falls Convention is held; Susan begins to fight for women's rights.

Susan works for women's property rights and suffrage.

Susan didn't pay the fine for a reason. She wanted her case to go to the **Supreme Court**. She wanted that court to rule on women's rights. But the judge let her case go. There was no court ruling.

Susan never stopped working for women's rights. In 1881, she began writing a book with Elizabeth. It's called *The History of Woman Suffrage*.

Susan (center) sits with other women's rights leaders.

Susan publishes *The Revolution* with Elizabeth.

Susan is arrested for voting.

1868 FEBRUARY 26, 1869 1872 1881 ADING . . .

Congress passes 15th Amendment: all males can vote.

Susan and Elizabeth write *The History of Woman Suffrage*.

27

Victory at Last

Susan B. Anthony died on March 13, 1906. For 60 years, she had fought for women's suffrage. When she died, she gave her money to the cause. It wasn't much. But 14 years later, her efforts paid off. On August 18, 1920, the 19th Amendment became law. It was called the Susan B. Anthony Amendment. At last, women had the right to vote.

Susan B. Anthony is born.

Susan joins anti-slavery group and teacher's union.

Susan hears Elizabeth speak; gives speeches for women's suffrage.

FEB. 15, 1820   1845   1848   JULY 1848   SEPT. 1852   1853

Susan gives speeches about temperance.

Seneca Falls Convention is held; Susan begins to fight for women's rights.

Susan works for women's property rights and suffrage.

Women watch as the governor of Kentucky signs to approve the 19th Amendment.

| Susan publishes *The Revolution* with Elizabeth. | Susan is arrested for voting. | Susan B. Anthony dies. |

| 1868 | FEBRUARY 26, 1869 | 1872 | 1881 | MAR. 13 1906 | 1920 |

| Congress passes 15th Amendment: all males can vote. | Susan and Elizabeth write *The History of Woman Suffrage.* | 19th Amendment gives women the right to vote. |

Glossary

amendment An addition to the United States Constitution voted on by Congress and agreed to by the states.

convention A formal meeting to discuss and act on things that concern a particular group.

petition A written request bearing the signatures of people who favor the request.

poll A place where people vote.

Quakers A Christian group, also called the Society of Friends, with strong political opinions on issues like slavery and equal rights for men and women.

suffrage The right to vote.

Supreme Court The highest court in the United States; it often makes decisions on major issues, like voting rights.

temperance The refusal to use alcohol or permit its use by others.

union An organized group of workers that protects and improves working conditions, wages, and health benefits.

Read More

Carson, Mary Kay. *Why Couldn't Susan B. Anthony Vote?: and other questions about . . . women's suffrage.* New York: Sterling, 2015.

Goddu, Krystyna Poray. *What's Your Story, Susan B. Anthony?* Minneapolis: Lerner, 2016.

Hannigan, Kate. *A Lady Has the Floor: Belva Lockwood Speaks Out for Women's Rights.* Honesdale, Penn.: Calkins Creek, 2018.

Websites

National Geographic Kids | Facts About the Suffragettes
https://www.natgeokids.com/uk/discover/history/general-history/suffragettes-facts/

Scholastic | Women's Suffrage
http://teacher.scholastic.com/activities/suffrage/index.htm

States and Territories that Allowed Women to Vote before the 19th Amendment
https://www.tolerance.org/sites/default/files/general/suffrage_map.pdf

Index

About the Author

Elizabeth Raum has written over 100 books for young readers. Many are biographies. She enjoys learning about people who help us see the world in new and exciting ways. She lives in Fargo, North Dakota. To learn more, visit her website: www.ElizabethRaumBooks.com.

Chapter 16

Stars and *Galaxies*

You Will Discover

- what tools people have used in the past and are using now to learn about the universe.
- the characteristics of stars.
- how stars are grouped.

online
Student Edition

pearsonsuccessnet.com

How has the study of stars expanded our knowledge of the universe?

light-year

black hole

A black hole is a point in space that has such a strong force of gravity that nothing within a certain distance of it can escape getting pulled into the black hole—not even light.

506

supernova

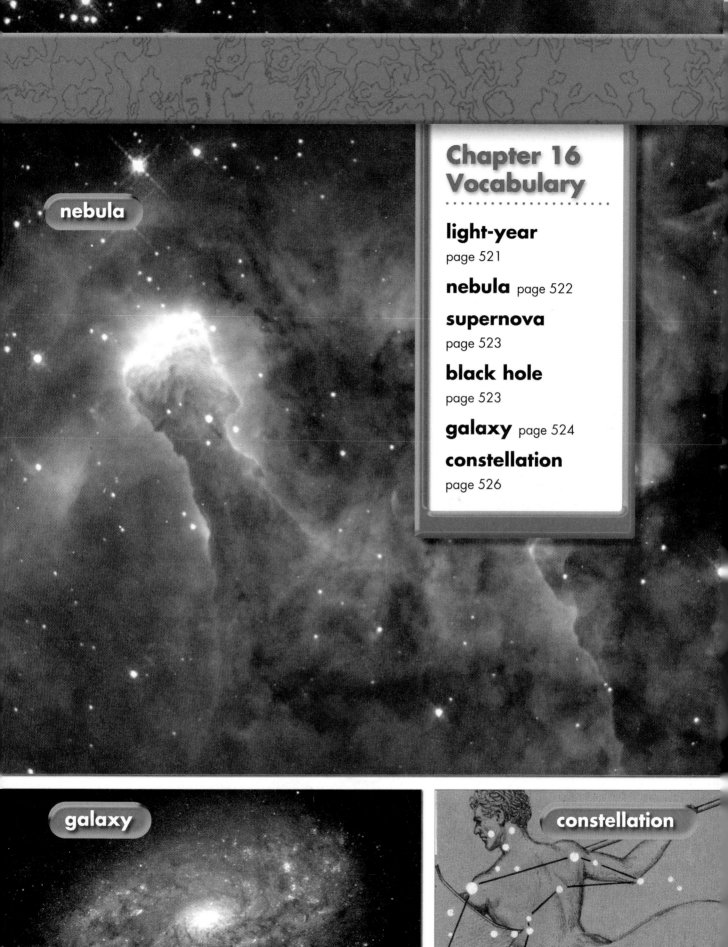

nebula

galaxy

constellation

507

Directed Inquiry

Explore How can you make an astrolabe?

Any astronomical tool that measures the angle of an object in the sky can be called an astrolabe. The astrolabe below is much simpler than a classic astrolabe.

Materials

Astrolabe Pattern and cardboard

glue and tape

scissors

straw

pencil

string and washer

Process Skills

Scientists **communicate** when they explain data or give an opinion, orally or in writing.

What to Do

1 Cut out the Astrolabe Pattern. Glue it onto cardboard. Cut off the extra cardboard.

Make a tiny hole with a dull pencil. Put the end of the string through the hole. Tape onto the back.

Make a tiny hole with a pencil.

Push the end of the string through the hole. Tape onto back.

Cut off extra straw

Astrolabe

Cut

Look through this end

straw

Never look at the Sun with your astrolabe.

Be careful!

85
80
75
70
65
60
55
50
45
40
35
30
25
20
15
10
5

Tape on a straw.

string
knot
washer

2 Look through your astrolabe at the paper star your teacher has placed in your room. Ask another student to read the angle where the string crosses the numbered scale.

Optional: Some star charts give the time, direction, and angle at which a star or planet can be found. If possible, use your astrolabe, a compass, and a watch to locate stars such as the North Star, constellations such as the Big Dipper, and planets such as Jupiter.

Explain Your Results

Communicate How does an astrolabe measure the angle of a star? Why did different students get different angles for the paper star?

How to Read Science

Reading Skills

TARGET SKILL
Summarize

A summary is a short retelling of something you have read. When you write a summary, include only the most important ideas. Leave out most details, and do not add any new ideas. Use your own words when you **summarize.**

Using a graphic organizer can help you organize and **communicate** the main ideas for your summary.

History Article

An astrolabe is used to tell time and direction. No one is sure when the astrolabe was invented. Its beginnings can be traced back to Greeks about 200 B.C. One of the first clear descriptions of an astrolabe, though, does not appear until about 400 A.D. Astrolabes continued to be developed over the centuries. Several different kinds were made and many were beautifully decorated. When pendulum clocks and other science instruments were developed in the 1600s, the use of astrolabes declined.

Apply It!

Read the history article. Use a graphic organizer like this one to choose ideas to include in your **summary**. Then write a two- or three-sentence summary to **communicate** the main ideas.

Information	Information	Information

Summary

509

You Are There!

It's early afternoon on a beautiful spring day. The Sun is out. The birds are tweeting and chirping. It's warm enough that you've taken off your jacket. But something seems wrong. The sky is getting darker, but there's not a cloud to be seen anywhere. It's way too early for sunset, but you notice you can see a few stars. The birds are silent. This scene feels very creepy. What exactly is going on here?

AudioText

What is the history of astronomy?

Ancient people kept a close watch on the Sun, Moon, and stars. They learned about them by using their eyes. Over centuries, people invented tools that helped them learn much more about the universe.

Patterns in the Sky

Patterns of events seen in the sky were very important to many cultures throughout history. Patterns are repeated events, such as the seasons, the phases of the Moon, and the rising and setting of the Sun each day. Long ago, people all over the world made calendars based on the predictable cycles in the sky.

The changing of seasons was very important to people around the world. People were interested in when to plant crops or hold festivals. Certain sets of stars were expected to appear in specific seasons. Anything that was different from the predictable cycles, such as appearances of new objects in the sky, were thought of as having special meanings.

Eclipses

A solar eclipse occurs when the Moon blocks the Sun's light. A lunar eclipse occurs when Earth casts a shadow on the Moon. Eclipses are rare events that were not part of the regular patterns seen in the sky. They were thought by ancient cultures to have special meanings, usually that something bad was going to happen. Knowing when an eclipse would occur was very helpful for leaders. They could make predictions only after they carefully observed and recorded the movements of the Sun and Moon. People in Asia, the Middle East, and South America have left records of their observations and predictions of eclipses.

1. ✔**Checkpoint** What is a solar eclipse? a lunar eclipse?
2. **Math in Science** Babylonian astronomers noted that eclipses of the Moon occur in a cycle that lasts 233 months. About how many years is that cycle?

Astronomy Around the World

Most ancient peoples left no written records of their observations of the sky. However, they did leave behind buildings and other structures that show how important the movements of the Sun, Moon, and stars were to them.

Stone Circles

The giant circle of stones known as Stonehenge that stands in a field in southwest England has puzzled scientists and historians for years. Ancient people started building Stonehenge more than 5,000 years ago. They worked on it on and off for over 1,500 years. Today, only parts of it remain. Originally, it consisted of an outer circle of 30 enormous upright blocks of stone. Other slabs of stone were laid horizontally on top to form a ring. Inside the circle was another smaller circle of about 60 stones and inside of it were more stones arranged in a horseshoe pattern.

Most scientists agree that the stone circles were linked to astronomy and that those who built Stonehenge had a good understanding of the cycle of the Sun and the seasons. For example, some of the stones point to the position in the sky where the Sun rises and sets on the longest day of the year. Other stones are arranged to mark the rising of the Sun or the Moon at other times during the year.

Ancient peoples in North America built stone circles similar to Stonehenge. One of the best known is the Big Horn Medicine Wheel, near Sheridan, Wyoming.

Chomsongdae Observatory on the Korean peninsula was built nearly 1,400 years ago. A hole at the top allowed people to view the stars and planets. Many similar observatories are found all over East Asia, but this one is the oldest.

Measured all the way across, Stonehenge is about one-third the length of a football field. Some stones weigh up to 50 tons and stand as tall as 9 meters (30 feet).

Pyramids

About 700 years ago in what is now Mexico, people built a large pyramid at a place called Chichén Itzá. This four-sided pyramid shows that the people were very clever sky watchers. Each of the pyramid's four sides has 91 steps. If you count the platform step at the top, the pyramid has 365 steps, the same as the number of days in one year. A special pattern appears in late afternoon on the spring and fall equinoxes, the time of year when day and night are of equal length. Shadows form a pattern that looks like a snake slithering down the stairway. The appearance of this pattern may have marked the date for special yearly ceremonies related to farming.

The pyramid at Chichén Itzá, in Mexico, is known as El Castillo. It is 24 meters (79 feet) tall, about twice as tall as a telephone pole.

1. ✔**Checkpoint** What did ancient peoples leave behind that tells us that the cycles of the Sun, Moon, and stars were important to them?
2. 🔄 **Summarize** what you have learned about the astronomical observations of ancient cultures.

Middle East Astronomy

Astronomy thrived in the Middle East for many centuries. Scholars from this region played an important role in early astronomy. One such person was Ulugh Beg (1394–1449). In 1420, he began building an observatory containing a huge sextant. The diameter was longer than six of today's school buses! Ulugh Beg used observations of the Sun to calculate the length of the year to within a minute of our current calculations. He also compiled a list of the exact locations of more than 1,000 stars.

Early Tools

People invented tools to help them better understand the stars. In Europe and the Middle East, the astrolabe was primarily used from about 200 B.C. to 1700 A.D. This tool consisted of a star map drawn on a metal plate. It had movable parts that allowed a viewer to measure the angle between the horizon and a star or planet. Other plates could be adjusted to show what the sky would look like at a particular time or place.

By the 1700s, the astrolabe had been replaced with other tools, such as the sextant. Like the astrolabe, a sextant measures the angle between the horizon and a point in the sky. However, a sextant consists of a movable arm, mirrors, and an eyepiece attached to a frame shaped like a piece of pie.

Astrolabes could be used to find the time, predict when the Sun would rise or set, or determine where certain stars would appear. Sailors used a type of astrolabe to find their position while at sea.

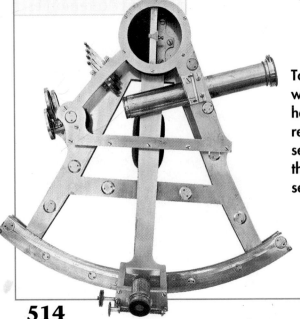

To find the angle of a star above the horizon, a person would line up the eyepiece of a sextant with the horizon. Then he would move the arm until the star was reflected by the mirrors on the sextant so that the star seemed to be lined up with the horizon. The angle could then be read from markings on the frame. Sailors used sextants to navigate by the stars.

Early Telescopes

The invention of the telescope, which gathers light to magnify faraway objects in the sky, was a breakthrough in astronomy. The Italian scientist Galileo Galilei (1564–1642) was the first person to use a telescope in astronomy, although he did not invent the telescope.

Galileo's telescopes were not very powerful. At best, they made an object look 20 times as large—about the same as one of today's beginner telescopes.

Galileo discovered that the Moon has mountains and that the Sun spins. He also discovered that Venus has phases like the Moon. One of Galileo's most important discoveries was that Jupiter has four moons that orbit around it.

In Galileo's day, many people believed that the Sun and the planets revolved around Earth. Galileo's discoveries led to the opposite conclusion—that the Earth and the other planets revolved around the Sun. Many people angrily refused to believe that the Earth was not the center of the universe. It would take years before Galileo's ideas were widely accepted.

The year Galileo died, 1642, another scientific genius was born. His name was Isaac Newton. Newton developed the reflecting telescope. Earlier telescopes used lenses to focus light and magnify distant objects. Newton's telescope used a curved mirror. It allowed people to see objects that were dimmer and farther away and to see the objects in sharper detail.

Early telescopes

1. **✓Checkpoint** What did Galileo conclude from his observations of Jupiter and Venus?

2. **Technology** in Science Use Internet or library resources to find when telescopes were used to see or photograph the objects Neptune, Uranus, and Pluto.

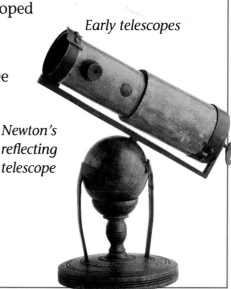

Newton's reflecting telescope

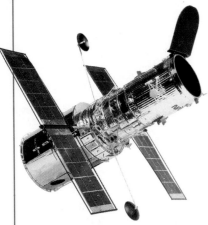

The Hubble Space Telescope detects ultraviolet waves, visible light, and infrared waves. Its cameras have photographed the planets in our solar system, the birth of new stars, and the fiery explosion that occurs near the end of a star's life.

Today's High-Tech Telescopes

Telescopes work because they gather light and concentrate it. The more light that reaches our eyes, the brighter an object will seem. The light we see coming from the Sun or the stars—visible light—is only a small fraction of the light energy in the universe. Most objects in space, including the Sun and other stars, emit a lot of electromagnetic radiation that we cannot see, including radio waves, infrared waves, ultraviolet waves, X rays, and gamma rays. Special telescopes have been developed that can detect different types of invisible radiation. The more types of radiation astronomers can study, the more they can learn about the universe.

Telescopes have become much bigger and much better since the time of Newton's reflecting telescope. For example, two huge twin telescopes, known as Keck I and Keck II, tie the record as the largest telescopes in the world. They each have a main mirror that measures 10 meters across. The mirrors are actually made out of 36 pieces that work together as a system to gather visible light and infared radiation. Astronomers use the Keck telescopes to study very distant stars.

Radio Telescopes

Telescopes that detect radio waves look more like satellite dishes than traditional telescopes. Instead of a mirror or lens, a bowl-shaped dish collects and focuses radio waves given off by distant objects in space. Radio telescopes often consist of multiple dishes arranged in a group, or array. The radio signals detected by the dishes in an array can be added together. An array of dishes is like one giant dish that is as large as the space covered by all the dishes in the array.

For telescopes to work well, they need very dark, clear night skies. Keck I and II were built on top of the dormant volcano Mauna Kea in Hawaii. They are located far from city lights, in areas where it is rarely cloudy at night.

Earth-based telescopes must view stars through the warm and cool air currents of the Earth's atmosphere. This can cause images to look fuzzy. Also, most types of electromagnetic radiation are partly or completely blocked by Earth's atmosphere. To get a more complete picture, some telescopes are launched into space where conditions are always clear and dark, perfect for stargazing around the clock! Space telescopes include the Hubble and the Chandra X-ray Observatory.

The Arecibo radio telescope in Puerto Rico is the largest single-dish radio telescope in the world. It receives radio waves from planets and stars as well as extremely distant objects called pulsars, which send out rapid-fire bursts of radio waves.

Radio waves bounce off the dish and hit the detector high above.

The dish is 305 meters (almost 1,000 feet) across, or about the length of three football fields.

✓Lesson Checkpoint

1. How are radio telescopes different from the Keck telescopes?
2. Why must certain types of telescopes be sent into space?
3. Writing in Science **Expository** Write a paragraph in your **science journal** explaining which of the ancient structures you read about in this lesson you would most like to visit, and what you would hope to see.

Lesson 2

What is a star?

There are hundreds of thousands of stars in this group of stars.

Take a look at the night-time sky and you'll see more stars than you could ever begin to count. They are different sizes, ages, colors, and distances from Earth.

How the Sun Stacks Up as a Star

The Sun is a star. Stars, including the Sun, are gigantic balls of very hot gases that give off electromagnetic radiation. As stars go, the Sun is not unusual at all. It is of medium size. Stars known as giants may be 8 to 100 times as large as the Sun. Supergiants are even larger. They may be up to 300 times as large as the Sun. Other stars are much smaller—only about the size of Earth. Compared to the Earth, though, the Sun is huge. If you think of the Sun as a gumball machine and the Earth as a gumball, it would take a million Earth gumballs to fill the Sun gumball machine.

The Sun gives off enormous amounts of thermal energy and light energy. These energies come from powerful reactions involving the Sun's two main components, hydrogen and helium gas. Deep inside the core of the Sun, the nuclei of hydrogen atoms have such a high temperature and kinetic energy that when they collide, they fuse together. The nuclei combine to form a new nucleus and a new element, helium. Huge amounts of energy are released as this happens, which is what makes the Sun shine.

There are many different sizes and colors of stars.

Brightness, Color, and Temperature of Stars

The Sun is the closest star to Earth. It is by far the brightest star in the sky. It's easy to think that the stars that look the brightest are the closest. However, Barnard's Star is the third closest to Earth, but it can't be seen without a telescope.

So just what is it that makes some stars look bright? The brightest stars are the stars that give off the most energy. But a star's size, temperature, and distance from Earth all play a part in how bright a star looks to us. The dazzling white star Sirius, for example, is the brightest star in the night sky, but it is only the ninth closest star to Earth. It is larger, hotter, and more than 20 times as bright as the Sun. It doesn't look brighter to us because it is much farther from us than the Sun. If we could line up all the stars at the same distance from Earth, we could see which stars are really the brightest.

A star's color tells you how hot it is. Red stars, like Barnard's Star are the coolest. Somewhat hotter are orange and yellow stars, like the Sun with a temperatures of about 5500°C. The hottest stars are white or blue-white. Even though red stars are said to be "cool," they are still extremely hot. Barnard's Star is about 2250° C (4000° F). At that temperature a piece of iron would melt instantly and boil away into a gas.

1. **✓ Checkpoint** Which star is hotter, a yellow star or a white star?

2. **Social Studies** in Science Many of the brightest stars were named long ago. Do some research to find out who named the bright stars Vega and Rigel and what their names mean.

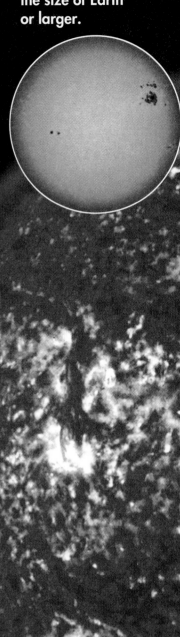

The Explosive Sun

The Sun is a fiery ball of hot gases with no hard surfaces. But astronomers have identified various layers of the Sun. The part of the Sun that gives off the light energy we see is called the photosphere. It is the innermost layer of the Sun's atmosphere. The layer above the photosphere is the chromosphere. The outermost layer is called the corona.

The Sun may look pretty calm—no more exciting than a giant glowing light bulb. But when scientists look at it with special telescopes and other equipment, they see a lot of activity. Galileo noticed dark spots moving along the face of the Sun and concluded that the Sun must be rotating. Today we know that these are sunspots, which are part of the photosphere. They look dark because they are not as hot as the rest of the photosphere. The way the sunspots travel across the face of the Sun indicates that the Sun rotates more slowly at its poles than at its equator.

The number of sunspots changes in cycles of about 11 years. Sometimes there are many, and sometimes there are few.

Sunspots may be the size of Earth or larger.

Solar Eruptions

Loops and fountains of blazing gases may leap out of the chromosphere, reaching hundreds of thousands of kilometers up into the corona. These ribbons of glowing gas are called prominences. Prominences may appear and then disappear in a few days or months.

Another explosive event linked to the sunspot cycle occurs when parts of the chromosphere erupt like a volcano. Such an "eruption" is called a solar flare. It causes a temporary bright spot in the chromosphere that may last for minutes or hours. A solar flare spews out huge amounts of electromagnetic waves, protons, and electrons into space. These waves and particles may interrupt radio communication and cause damage to electrical systems.

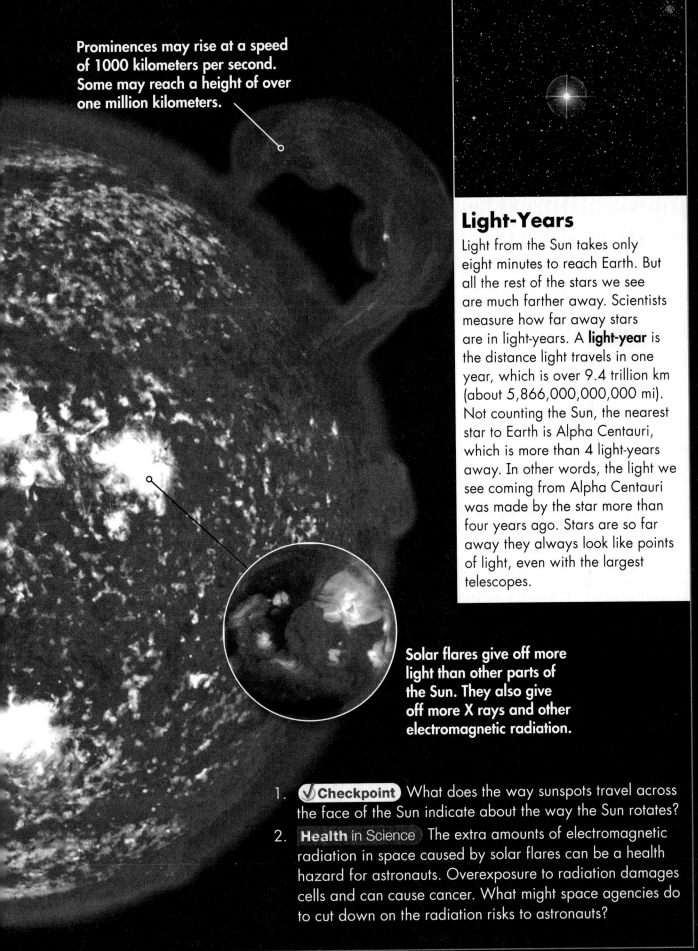

Prominences may rise at a speed of 1000 kilometers per second. Some may reach a height of over one million kilometers.

Light-Years

Light from the Sun takes only eight minutes to reach Earth. But all the rest of the stars we see are much farther away. Scientists measure how far away stars are in light-years. A **light-year** is the distance light travels in one year, which is over 9.4 trillion km (about 5,866,000,000,000 mi). Not counting the Sun, the nearest star to Earth is Alpha Centauri, which is more than 4 light-years away. In other words, the light we see coming from Alpha Centauri was made by the star more than four years ago. Stars are so far away they always look like points of light, even with the largest telescopes.

Solar flares give off more light than other parts of the Sun. They also give off more X rays and other electromagnetic radiation.

1. **Checkpoint** What does the way sunspots travel across the face of the Sun indicate about the way the Sun rotates?

2. **Health** in Science The extra amounts of electromagnetic radiation in space caused by solar flares can be a health hazard for astronauts. Overexposure to radiation damages cells and can cause cancer. What might space agencies do to cut down on the radiation risks to astronauts?

521

The Life of Stars

Thanks to powerful telescopes, scientists have glimpsed new stars being born and ancient stars dying. New stars form in a cloud of gas and dust called a **nebula.** As particles of gas and dust churn around, gravity begins to pull together a clump of particles into a ball. Gravity increases in the ball, and more and more particles are pulled in. At the same time, the temperature rises. If it gets hot enough, hydrogen will begin changing into helium and releasing tremendous amounts of energy. The massive and dense clump of particles will officially have become a star.

Stars live an extremely long time, but they don't live forever. In billions of years, the Sun will use up all of the hydrogen (its "fuel") in its core. It will become several thousand times brighter and expand to about 170 times its current size—about out to where Mars orbits now.

In this photograph, stars are seen forming and dying.

This star is about to have a supernova. The ring and nearby clouds are debris ejected from the star's poles and equator.

These are young stars.

These fingers of gas and dust are part of the Eagle Nebula, which is 7,000 light-years away. Inside these dusty towers, new stars are forming.

Stars are forming in these clouds.

As the Sun expands, its temperature will be slightly cooler, so it will be red, rather than yellow. It will be known as a red giant star. At this point, it will be using helium as fuel. When the helium is used up, the core will shrink to about the size of Earth. The remaining layers of gas will float off into space. The core will become a white dwarf star. A white dwarf has no fuel to convert to radiant energy. The leftover thermal energy from its energy-producing days keeps the star hot for a long time. Over several million years, a white dwarf cools down and becomes a cold object called a black dwarf.

Massive stars go out in a blaze of glory. When a massive star's core runs out of fuel, it starts shrinking until it can shrink no farther. Powerful shock waves from this sudden stop fan outward, and particles of matter spin off into space carrying huge amounts of energy with them. A gigantic explosion occurs that is millions or billions of times as bright as the star ever was. This explosion is known as a **supernova.** It hurls matter and energy far out into space. Usually, all that will be left behind is a ball of neutrons that is about 20 km (12 mi) across. This city-sized object is called a neutron star.

If the core was quite massive—more massive than three Suns—the core's own gravity will keep causing it to shrink until it becomes a black hole. A **black hole** is a point in space that has such a strong force of gravity that nothing within a certain distance of it can escape getting pulled into the black hole—not even light.

✓ Lesson Checkpoint

1. What is the Sun?
2. Where does a new star form?
3. ↻ Summarize the three ways a star might die.

At the center of this nebula, two stars orbit each other. One of the stars is dying and has thrown off most of its gas layers, creating this butterfly-shaped cloud of gas and dust.

How are stars grouped together?

Ancient people divided the sky up into groups of stars. This made studying the stars easier. Today we know that the stars— including the Sun—are part of even larger groupings of stars that are all bound to each other by gravity.

Galaxies

The Sun, the Earth, and the other planets in the solar system are part of the galaxy known as the Milky Way. A **galaxy** is a huge system of stars, dust, and gas held together by gravity. There are billions of galaxies in the universe. A few can be seen without a telescope, but they are so far away they look like single points of light. Using powerful telescopes, astronomers have learned that galaxies come in different shapes and sizes.

About three-fourths of the galaxies that have been discovered are spiral galaxies. They look like pinwheels. They have bright, bulging middles and wispy arms that fan out from the center. The stars in the arms of the galaxy are circling the center bulge of the galaxy, much as the Earth moves around the Sun.

Elliptical galaxies can be almost round or more oval like a football. The largest galaxies we know of are elliptical. There are also elliptical galaxies that are many times smaller than our galaxy.

Some galaxies are neither spiral nor elliptical. Galaxies that have no real shape are called irregular galaxies. Irregular galaxies are probably young galaxies in which stars are still forming.

1. ✓**Checkpoint** What type of galaxy is the Milky Way?
2. **Math in Science** Look at the spiral galaxy that was photographed by the Hubble telescope on page 525. About how many times farther away is this galaxy than the Small Magellenic Cloud?

SciLinks Take It to the Net
pearsonsuccessnet.com | keyword: galaxy
code: g5p524

Approximate location of our solar system.

This side view of the Milky Way shows the bright bulging middle and wispy arms of this spiral galaxy. Our solar system is toward the end of one of the Milky Way's arms, about 25,000 to 30,000 light-years from the center.

It is easy to see why a spiral galaxy is known as a "sombrero galaxy." The center of the galaxy is giving off huge quantities of X rays, which astronomers think may mean that a gigantic black hole lies at the heart of the galaxy.

This irregular galaxy is called the Small Magellanic Cloud. This young galaxy is about 200,000 light-years away from Earth and is orbiting the Milky Way.

This photo of a spiral galaxy was taken by cameras on the Hubble Space Telescope. It is about 60 million light-years away. The center of the galaxy contains older yellow and red stars. The arms contain large amounts of dust and young, hot blue stars.

All galaxies are constantly moving through space. In several billion years, these two spiral galaxies will run into each other, and the smaller galaxy will be incorporated into the larger galaxy.

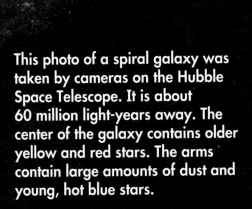

Constellations

In the past, people looked up at the night sky and "connected the dots" formed by the stars. They saw patterns that reminded them of bears, dogs, a swan, a lion, and even a sea monster! Today, scientists divide the night sky into 88 constellations. A **constellation** is a group of stars that forms a pattern. A map of constellations is like a map with outlines drawn around all the states of the United States. Many constellation names are the names of the star patterns people used long ago.

Dividing the sky into sections makes studying stars easier. A constellation is a little like a star's address. For example, if you tell the state you live in, people know where in the country you live. Knowing which constellation a star is in lets you know where in the sky to look to find that star.

Two stars that seem close together in the same constellation may not really be close. One star may be billions of kilometers farther from Earth than the other. They appear to be close together because they are in the same direction from Earth.

People who live in different parts of Earth see different sections of the sky and different constellations. The half of Earth north of the equator is called the Northern Hemisphere. The half to the south is called the Southern Hemisphere. The United States is in the Northern Hemisphere. Ursa Major can be seen in the Northern Hemisphere. But people in the Southern Hemisphere cannot see it.

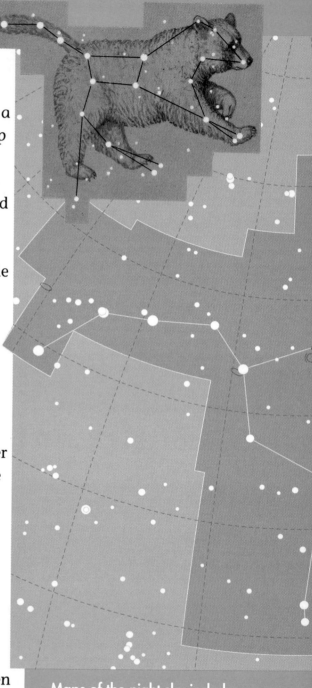

In the constellation Ursa Major, the Big Dipper forms the bear's back and its tail.

Maps of the night sky include imaginary lines around each constellation. The constellation of Ursa Major, shown here at the top of the page, includes the pattern of stars that gives the constellation its name and all the other stars within the imaginary lines.

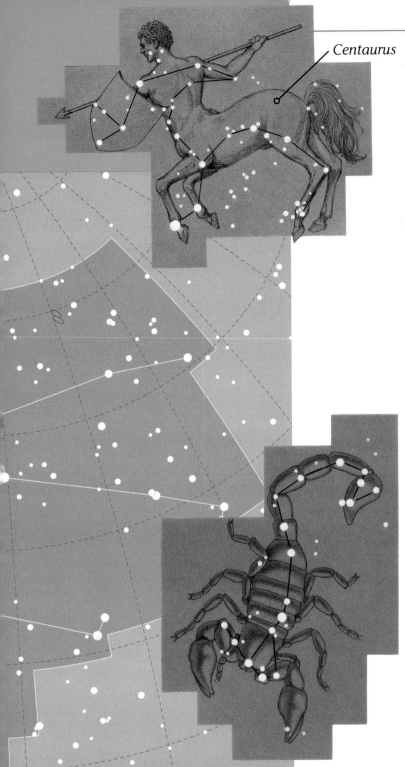

Centaurus

The constellation Centaurus can be seen only from the Southern Hemisphere. It is named after a character in an ancient Greek myth who was half human and half horse. It has a bright, triple-star system with the three closest stars to the Sun. They are in one of Centaurus's legs.

The ancient Greeks named another constellation Scorpius because they thought the group of stars looked like a scorpion— a small creature with a tail that delivers a painful or deadly sting. If you look at Scorpius through a telescope, you will see that many of the bright points of light are not single stars but large clusters of stars. The brightest single star in the constellation is the red supergiant Antares, which lies near the center of the scorpion's "body."

Ancient Greeks thought this star group looked like a scorpion.

1. ✓**Checkpoint** Which constellation is the Big Dipper in?

2. **Social Studies** in Science The Big Dipper had special meaning for African American slaves in the South before the Civil War. A song called "Follow the Drinking Gourd" told slaves how following the Big Dipper would lead them North to freedom. Use the Internet or library resources to find out why the Big Dipper served as a good guide.

527

The Big Dipper Today

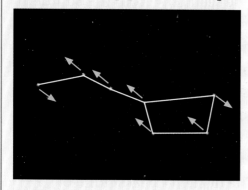

The arrows show how the stars of the Big Dipper are moving relative to one another.

The Big Dipper in 100,000 years

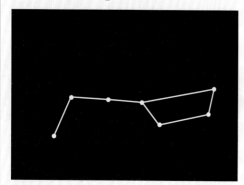

Tens of thousands of years from now, the Big Dipper will look much different. Its handle will look more crooked and the bowl more stretched out because the star at the end of the handle and the star at the far top of the bowl will have moved in opposite directions. What will the Big Dipper look like in 200,000 years?

Stars on the Move

Stars do not always appear in the same place in the sky. They move in logical and predictable ways. Suppose you looked at the sky early one evening and found the Big Dipper. When you looked two hours later, the Big Dipper seemed to have moved toward the western horizon. Actually, the Big Dipper did not move, but you moved. Every 24 hours, Earth makes one complete rotation. This spinning of Earth is why the Sun seems to travel across the sky every day—rising in the east and setting in the west. It is also why the stars appear to move across the sky in the same direction.

Seasonal Changes

Ursa Major, which contains the Big Dipper, is visible all year. But other constellations can be seen only at certain times of the year. In the United States, you can see the constellation Canis Major, or the Great Dog, only in winter. Constellations change with the seasons because Earth is traveling around the Sun. It takes Earth one year to travel around the Sun. As Earth makes its journey, people see different parts of the sky at night. In a way, it's like riding a merry-go-round. As you look outward during a ride, you see different parts of your surroundings.

Nothing in the universe stands still. Stars move through space in various directions and at various speeds. We cannot see them move because the stars are so very far away. But over very long periods of time, the patterns of stars will change as some stars move closer to or farther away from each other.

Seasonal Changes in the Sky

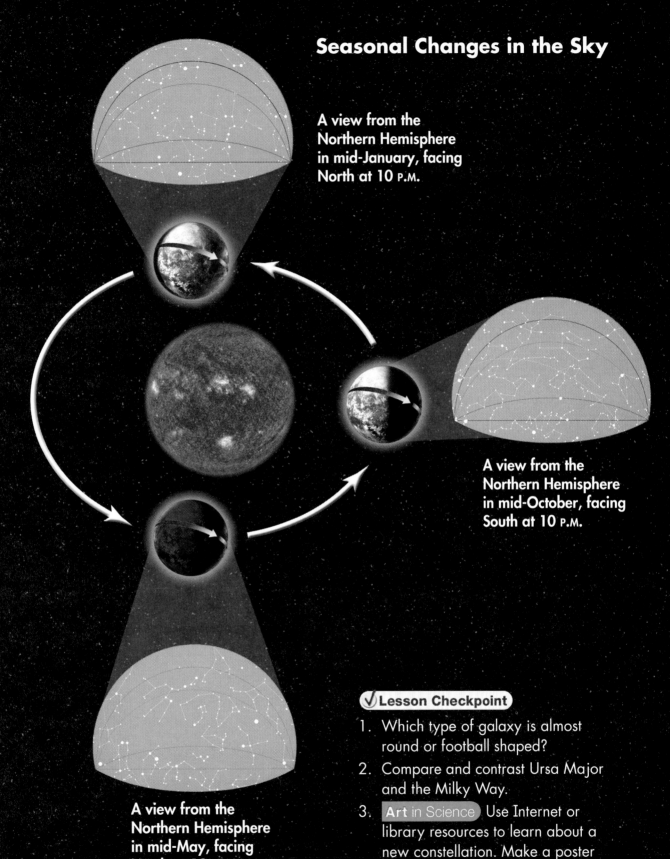

A view from the Northern Hemisphere in mid-January, facing North at 10 P.M.

A view from the Northern Hemisphere in mid-October, facing South at 10 P.M.

A view from the Northern Hemisphere in mid-May, facing North at 10 P.M.

✓ Lesson Checkpoint

1. Which type of galaxy is almost round or football shaped?

2. Compare and contrast Ursa Major and the Milky Way.

3. **Art** in Science Use Internet or library resources to learn about a new constellation. Make a poster about your constellation that includes a drawing and information about it.

Investigate What does a spiral galaxy look like from different angles?

Our solar system is located near the edge of the Milky Way. The Milky Way is called a spiral galaxy because it is shaped like a spiral.

Materials

25 cups

What to Do

1 **Make a model** of a spiral galaxy.

2 **Observe** the cups from directly above the table. This view represents the galaxy as seen from outside the galaxy. Draw a sketch or diagram of what you see.

3 Kneel beside the cups on the edge of the table. Look across the table at the other side of the cups. This view represents the galaxy as seen from a planet near the galaxy's edge.

These cups represent a spiral galaxy.

Process Skills

You **make a model** when you use representations to explain ideas.

4 Draw a diagram of what you see.

Model of a Spiral Galaxy	
View from Above	**View from the Edge**

Explain Your Results

1. How did the angle from which you viewed your **model** affect what you saw?

2. How is the model like a spiral galaxy? How is it different?

3. **Predict** Suppose you made a model of an elliptical galaxy. When seen from above, would it look the same as a spiral galaxy? When seen from the edge, would it look the same as a spiral galaxy? Test your predictions.

Our Sun is a star near the edge of the Milky Way, a spiral galaxy.

Go Further

If possible in your area, observe stars in the night sky. Use a sky chart to help find our galaxy, the Milky Way. Also try to identify stars in the night sky that are unusually bright or ones that appear slightly red or blue.

Shrinking the Universe Down to Size

Most things in the universe are very large. Even in our own solar system, it is hard to understand the size of our Sun, the other stars, and the planets.

To make large sizes and great distances easier to understand, it is helpful to shrink them down. In the chart, the comparative diameters are in centimeters to help you see how the sizes compare.

Star	Approximate Diameter	Comparative Diameter
Sun	1,400,000 km	1.4 cm
Beta Pegasi (a giant star)	133,000,000 km	133 cm
Hadar B (a giant star)	16,800,000 km	16.8 cm
Arcturus (a giant star)	35,000,000 km	35 cm
Sirius A (a main sequence star)	2,660,000 km	2.66 cm

Use the table on page 532 to answer the questions.

1. Which star shown has a diameter that is almost twice the Sun's diameter?
   A. Beta Pegasi
   B. Arcturus
   C. Sirius A
   D. Hadar B

2. Which star shown is almost 100 times as large as the Sun?
   F. Sirius A
   G. Hadar B
   H. Arcturus
   I. Beta Pegasi

3. The planet Jupiter has a diameter of about 140,000 km. It is about $\frac{1}{10}$ the size of which star?
   A. the Sun
   B. Beta Pegasi
   C. Hadar B
   D. Sirius A

4. List the 5 stars in the chart in order from smallest to largest.

Lab zone Take-Home Activity

Make a model of the 5 stars listed in the table on page 532. Use paper cut-outs to make your models. Tape several pieces of paper together to make the larger star models.

Chapter 16 Review and Test Prep

Use Vocabulary

black hole (page 523)	**light-year** (page 521)
constellation (page 526)	**nebula** (page 522)
galaxy (page 524)	**supernova** (page 523)

Use the term from the list above that best completes each sentence.

1. A huge system of stars, dust, and gas held together by gravity is a(n)_____.

2. A point in space that has such a strong force of gravity that nothing within a certain distance of it can escape is known as a(n)_____.

3. A group of stars that forms a pattern is called a(n) _____.

4. A gigantic explosion that occurs near the end of the life of some stars is a(n) _____.

5. Stars form in a cloud called a(n) _____.

6. The distance light travels in one year is a(n) _____.

Explain Concepts

7. Explain two factors that affect how bright a star appears in the night sky.

8. Explain what a sunspot is and the pattern that exists in the number of sunspots that are observed.

9. Explain two reasons for sending telescopes into space.

10. Why do stars appear to move across the sky during the night?

Process Skills

11. **Classify** Suppose you are viewing two galaxies through a telescope. The first galaxy you look at has a bright center and curved arms. The second galaxy is oval. Classify the two galaxies.

12. **Interpret the data** in the chart below. Which of the stars listed is closest to our solar system? Which is farthest?

Name of star	Distance
Arcturus	37 light-years
Altair	17 light-years
Betelgeuse	425 light-years
Sirius	9 light-years

13. **Infer** Barnard's Star is the third closest star to Earth, but it can't be seen without a telescope. Sirius is the ninth closest star to Earth and the brightest star in the night sky. Although it is farther away, what can you infer about Sirius's size and temperature that would explain why it looks brighter than Barnard's Star?

MindPoint Quiz Show

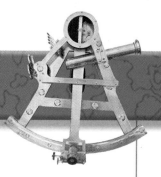

 Summarize

14. Make a graphic organizer like the one shown below. Use the details in the boxes to write a summary about the Sun's atmosphere.

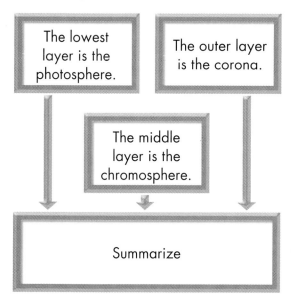

The lowest layer is the photosphere.

The outer layer is the corona.

The middle layer is the chromosphere.

Summarize

Test Prep

Choose the letter that best completes the statement or answers the question.

15. Watching the movements of the Sun, Moon, and stars was important to ancient cultures because it helped them
  Ⓐ predict the seasons and know when to plant crops.
  Ⓑ see better at night.
  Ⓒ build large stone monuments and observatories.
  Ⓓ discover spots on the face of the Sun.

16. A constellation is
  Ⓕ a system of stars, gas, and dust held together by gravity.
  Ⓖ a group of stars that forms a pattern.
  Ⓗ the largest kind of star.
  Ⓘ a set of telescopes on a mountain in Hawaii.

17. A light-year is
  Ⓐ the amount of time it takes light from the Sun to reach Earth.
  Ⓑ the distance from one end of the Milky Way to the other end.
  Ⓒ the distance light travels in one year.
  Ⓓ the amount of energy released when the Sun changes hydrogen into helium.

18. Galileo's discoveries
  Ⓕ helped him invent the telescope.
  Ⓖ provided evidence that the Earth and the planets revolve around the Sun.
  Ⓗ helped him realize that a better telescope could be made by using mirrors to gather light instead of lenses.
  Ⓘ helped him learn about the planets Neptune and Uranus.

19. Explain why the answer you select for Question 18 is best. For each of the answers you do not select, give a reason why it is not the best choice.

20. Writing in Science **Narrative**
Choose one way a star dies and write a death scene. Use dialogue, a setting, and the star as the main character.

Caroline Herschel
1750–1848

When Caroline Herschel officially became an astronomer in 1787, few women were ever paid for their work. Her salary, from the king of England, was low. But over time, her work made her famous.

Caroline Herschel was the assistant to her brother William Herschel. William had already achieved great fame with his discovery of the planet Uranus, in 1781. Caroline helped William make powerful telescopes. She also helped him record his nightly observations. She worked on the complex math needed to identify each object in the night sky.

William gave Caroline her own telescope. When she wasn't helping her brother, she made her own observations. Caroline discovered eight new comets. She tracked the positions of more than 500 stars that other astronomers had overlooked. She also discovered nebulas and observed star clusters and galaxies. Astronomers still use her star catalogs today.

Caroline Herschel worked as an astronomer until she was almost 80 years old. She received gold medals for her work and was invited to the palaces of kings and queens. Members of a German royal family came to visit her on her 97th birthday. She entertained them by singing. Her spirit was as bright as the stars she loved to study.

Lab zone Take-Home Activity

Use a book or ask an adult to help you find the constellation Orion, in the winter sky. Three bright stars form Orion's belt. Three dimmer stars below this belt make up Orion's sword. Use binoculars to find the nebula in Orion's sword.